Good-bye to the Sugar Refinery

Patience Wheatley

Goose Lane Editions

Some of these poems have appeared in *Antigonish Review, Canadian Woman Studies, Event, Germination, Green's Magazine, Matrix, Poetry Canada Review, Quarry,* and *Room of One's Own.*

Published by Goose lane Editions Ltd, 248 Brunswick Street, Fredericton, New Brunswick, Canada, E3B 1G9, 1989, with the assistance of the Canada Council and the University of New Brunswick.

Book design by Julie Scriver

Cover painting "Willie's Bouquet" by Susan Wanklyn, 1983, courtesy of the Hamilton Fish Collection

Canadian Cataloguing in Publication Data

Wheatley, Patience 1924-
Good-bye to the sugar refinery

Poems.
ISBN 0-86492-089-X

I. Title.

PS8595.H42G66 1989 C811'.54 C89-098518-9
PR9199.3.W53G66 1989

for David, William, Virginia, Susan

Willie's Bouquet

Our Willie
who loves orchids
left us
went to live among hibiscus
and morning glories.
Christmas he sent a gift of orchids, but
half-dead chrysanthemums appeared
a far cry from
hanging splendour of fringed open throats
yellow stamens
purple scented petals
of the cattleyas
he imagined

But the orchids live
as paint on canvas
and on the cover of this book.

Contents

PART 3 — A LAMP OF EARTH

PART 4 — GOOD-BYE TO THE SUGAR REFINERY

PART 1 — MADAME JANUS

Madame Janus

On the windswept
way station
with pillbox shelter
it's not just a matter of which side you stand
whether you go back or forward —

a trombone call
sounds closer, closer
and from the hole under the bridge
from the future
or the past
leaps the train with
three glittering eyes,
slows, shuts off its lights
slides along the platform.

Charon, in conductor's hat
helps me to NO
SMOKING — admonitory voice
welcomes me to Rapido
then the rhythm of the wheels
swings me away from
the city I've left —
having never come.

In spite of myself
I like the sight of
black furrows
shrugging through snow.
Surely I never saw before
this meandering river
and this spiralling hawk
hanging in currents of warm air.

And now I can't recall
gun emplacement architecture
grey presbyterianism —
don't know
whether I'm going in or out
to past or future.

Subject In Search Of Copula

Predicate n. (logic) What is predicated; affirmed or denied of the subject by means of the copula (e.g. "a fool" in "he is a fool"); (gram.) ,what is said of the subject, including the copula (e.g. "is a fool" in preceding example) . . .

Oxford Illustrated Dictionary

When young I confused love with
disappointment
Not recognising my
bondage
to romance
I reached a peak of ecstasy
when abandoned —
enraptured by a lover's cruelty
as much as the manna from his lips —
I mean
his lying silken words

Always coming back for more
I rattled my chain till
knocked down
for the third or fourth time I
cut loose
to marriage, children
discovering
(almost too late —
ah, blessed revelation!)

love is
the predicate

Glass Houses 1 — The Indoor Tennis Club

Winter tennis:
was like jumping into a spring-fed lake
on a hot summer day — the exhilaration of cold,
the slow-building heat of our effort.
Above, the vaulted roof groaned with snow
and pocked with heavy drops the red clay underneath.
And Mrs. C. who was over ninety and half blind
hit where she saw the ball was aimed,
steady as Gibraltar.

Now they're threatening
to pull down our delicate shelter — though we were
there on men's sufferance —
divorces, separations, deaths
and love gone wrong
were soothed in the hot cave of our locker room —
you could even have lunch if you liked,
at ten in the morning, or a first drink of gin
before going home to grapple
with a husband of seventy, a son of fifteen.

In the cold mornings, twenty below zero outside,
we were warm under our
crackling delicate roof.

He Said He Was Sorry

They were shocked
when she agreed
to “before and after” photos
for a congress of surgeons

if she could first
see the “before”
how the windscreen had shredded her face

Why not?   she said
It is just a mask of blood

She seemed to be
pleased at how they had fixed her up.
Didn’t seem to mind
being blind in one eye.

I wondered what else
inside her had shrivelled
besides the eye
that was fed with
blood but had lost
its function
  had lost
its nervous connection
  could not see
what had happened
  could not see it was dead.

After all   she said
he said he was sorry

Demonstrating The Underworld

We were prospectors
picking with forceps
in the deep trench
of the first cut in the shoulder
where grey fibres of flesh
stiff with formaldehyde
held threads of scarlet latex arteries.
Gingerly we dug deeper
flicking bits to the lab floor.

As soon as I saw the demonstrator
I knew Mephistopheles.
He seemed to have sprung from the underworld,
loping down the length
of the lab like a cat,
as if swinging a thick tail —
with pointed teeth
shining in his mouth.

Exuding the bitter chill of hell
he stood close
come to teach us
forbidden secrets —
yet warmth passed
from lab coat to lab coat
through the thick insulation
of love and learning
to the heart.

The Gesture
for Emily Carr

Watching ice
shrugging long pleats
in its pocked skin
across a mile of lake
I echo the gesture of painting
wondering how Emily Carr would have done it

her swirling brush strokes
would herd the ice
into great shrieking jams

I hear her pain
breaking up the frozen years.

Punch Lines

He couldn't punch his way out of a
paper bag
they used to say
of milquetoast boxers

He couldn't knock the skin off a
rice pudding

Punching your way
out of a paper bag
ain't easy, let me tell you
it's like
punching against the limp walls
of a woman's life

Remember
foolscap envelopes of law
shrivelled skin of prejudice?

Paper bags can be nightmares —
rice puddings, prisons!

Nightshade

She showed me
a cluster of shining red berries — what
are they? she asked
but then went on about
poetry

I don't know why
we started talking about
a sick friend
an orphaned child

the acorns fell onto the wooden deck
with sharp pings
like drips from icicles
on a sunny day
in winter

suddenly she said
she was so tired

the grove where we sat
eating fruit and cheese
with glasses of wine
was dappled with late
summer sunshine

She didn't seem to notice
the strong smell
that I smelt

I knew then
it was her
fear.

In An Old Limestone House At Belleville

we keep
the flowered curtain drawn
against cold

pull back the curtain
so I can see starlight

all the dark misery
of old stones gathers
between these walls
where winter hoar frost once
whitened the corners
and women with water-wrinkled hands
laboured under quilts that were histories of families —
got and delivered children
every particle of beauty in their faces
dried up by red hot stoves
and terror
of winter homelessness.

I need
to look out at old starlight
to see the world spinning forward.

PART 2 — W-40182

The Canadian Women's Army Corps came into being on 30 July 1941. Recruiting began in September 1941. By 31 December 1941, 1,256 women had enlisted or been appointed. On 13 March 1942 the CWAC was named a Corps of the Active Militia; CWAC officers then assumed Army Ranks and badges of rank.

W-40182 served in the CWAC from June 1943 to December 1945 when, after eighteen months service overseas, she was discharged in Montreal.

"The formation of the Canadian Women's Army Corps was one of the most striking innovations of Canadian military policy in the Second Great War. No one acquainted with the facts will deny that it was also one of the most successful."

The Canadian Army 1939-1945
C.P. Stacey, p.50

I — Recruit

Purpose

This is the season for
memories
when yellow leaves are etched
with insects' tunnels

recalling crunching patterns
made by our feet on parade ground gravel
to sharp words of command

until our precision squad marched
without directions
like a silky engine
like two champions skating
with a single purpose
a single brain

and if we're old and coarse now
and the patterns have led us far afield
let's remember the crunch of our feet
on the parade ground

when once we did it
together and
perfectly

June 1943

Recruit

We're waiting
to go to Kitchener for Basic Training

and at St. Sulpice Barracks of the C.W.A.C.
the Montreal Star
takes pictures of us
skiing down a mountain slope
just three feet high
to show that Cwacs have
outdoor exercise and
fun and
the friend I joined up with
laughs out from the poster on the
recruiting station wall
from under a tin hat —
released from scrubbing floors for
publicity shots
and even if her blonde curls are
too long and touch her
battledress collar
it's permitted for the good cause of
recruiting

Company night we're all C.B.ed for
movies
about V.D. and "Desert Victory" —

and then a film about
Service Women
having their hair styled
and uniforms fitted —
experimenting with discreet makeup.

Some of us
carry flags for Victory Loan
and are rewarded with
a ride around the city in an open truck
on a Saturday afternoon
from which I see
another friend in white bridal satin
the groom in khaki
on the steps of the fraternity house
where once I went
dancing

August 1943
#3 CWAC (Basic) Training Centre, Kitchener, Ontario.

There it is —
the army camp
and the huge gravelled square
with platoons marching
and Nissen huts
furnished with iron double-deckers

we shared our hut
with West Indians
training for the British A.T.S.
who didn't mind the blinding heat
of the mid-day parade ground
and the Corporal Instructors
telling us we were lucky
to be there in summer

at night
our Corporals put on
purple or green chenille housecoats
undid their rolled-up hair
sang in close harmony with
clear-voiced recruits from Cape Breton Island . . .
"There's a long, long trail awinding
unto the land of my dreams . . .
where the nightingale is singing
and a pale moon beams . . . "

while on the other side of our H hut
the West Indians
sang calypsos

and shocked our Canadian respectability
by putting a little brown girl
up on a table
who swivelled her hips and shoulders
leading rowdy choruses of
"Rum and Coca-cola . . . "

Some of the women of Kitchener
spat at us
while we route-marched.

September 1943
La Tuque, Quebec.

To La Tuque
a northern pulp and paper town
with wooden sidewalks
the army comes recruiting

6 of us Cwacs
a colour-party
in well-pressed khaki
carrying limp Canadian flags
march against scarlet and orange maples
burning on close hillsides

Later, in the school gymnasium
we sing "O Canada",
the Commanding Officer
with red face and lapel tabs
hands out testimonials and posthumous medals
to mothers of the dead

"Two sons killed," sobs a grey woman.
And the general
squeezes her hand, and looks
desperately round for help
not given
until the band strikes up Colonel Bogey
and we lift our flags and lead the parade
out into the smell of cedars
and the crackling Northern night
where Venus blazes
over threatening humps
of rank after rank of mountains.

Summer 1944
Messes

The Officers' mess at St. Sulpice Barracks
(coolly verandahed for summer drinking
overlooking a grassy yard and trees)
is Out-of-Bounds for Other Ranks:

we're confined to canteens,
ablution rooms and nit parades,
kit inspections,
double-deckers, barrack boxes, food from
chipped enamel pans on trestle tables
where each day the Duty Officer comes inquiring
"Any complaints?"

Meltzer's eaten her own
sardines
five times this week because of pork
Hebert doesn't like herrings
O'Rourke thinks the macaroni disgusting
and Tremblay's found
a cockroach
baked into a pie

Evenings
we sit beside the canteen's
small open window
hearing clinking glasses, voices, laughter
from the officers' verandah
and we gossip about their romances —
with married Captain this and Major that

And our Company Commander
living out a fantasy we've all had
takes unauthorized leave to go to Halifax
with her departing lover —

and is replaced

September 1944
Butchers

At the Hillside Ordnance Depot
they laugh at stories
of backstreet butchers
with their cohorts of taxi drivers
who'll do you an abortion anytime

Only when Corporal Tonks
comes screaming into the canteen
for Piché
collapsed on the stairs
and bleeding everywhere
and Miss Bijou sends you
racing after the taxi for the address

and the sickbay Sergeant
sends down for more towels
and later
you hear an ambulance howling
to our door
and then nothing more —

And when you hear it whispered
she's having penicillin
and still sinking
and her mother's sent for
you remember
how she came from Charlevoix County
excited about a new city-life in the army —

evenings in the canteen with girlfriends
clapping their hands and stamping
in time to a fiddler on the radio
ta-ta-tum, ta-ta-tum, ta-ta-tum . . .

October 1944

Overseas Draft

October and
Kitchener again —

the Overseas Draft
sequestered
behind the sergeants' mess
busily sewing canvas covers
for private luggage

not knowing when we leave
or even who is going
as signallers and drivers
are taken off the draft.

In reduced numbers
— not allowed to talk to others —
we visit
Kitchener's movie house
have dinner (once) at the hotel

pass segregated days
with medicals and needles
special kit parades
where we receive
khaki bloomers,
corsets (for support)

we gossip and write letters
to the sound of hoarse Corporal Instructors
putting new recruits through paces
we've forgotten

until with
sick uncertain feelings
hefting kit bags
thinking of home

we mount the Ocean Limited
laughing together
in frosty November dawn

November 1944

Convoy

We were three weeks
in a small ship on the North Atlantic —
forty seasick Cwacs
lurching through
military footdrill on a heaving deck
with the wind whipping up our skirts
and those RAF officers
watching.

Nothing but
slowly rolling ships
as far as anyone can see
with grey corvettes
heeling dangerously
darting at the convoy's edges
whooping horns
lamps blinking wildly from mast tops
to signal reassurance — warning —
how are we to know which?

especially when the ship behind
goes suddenly mad with signals
still unexplained
when we
go below to the bar
to fraternize with the RAF —
boyfriends by mid-Atlantic.

Coming down the Channel
(where excited middle-aged Colonels,
getting into the war at last,
man anti-aircraft guns)
we all have RAF fiancés.

Those signals from the ship astern —
are from their wives.

II — Addison Road, London W8.

By the end of 1943 there were 3 CWAC companies in London, England, with personnel attached for duty to various branches of Canadian Military Headquarters. 1,984 all ranks of the CWAC served overseas in the European zone between November 1942, when the first CWAC draft arrived in the U.K., and 8 May 1945, V.E. day.

The CWAC barracks on Addison Road, Kensington, were spread out up and down the road. One house contained the switchboard, mess, officers' mess, kitchens and Orderly Room. The other houses were dormitories. Most of the Other Ranks worked at Canadian Military Headquarters Records Office, Acton.

January 1945
Addison Road, Kensington — 50 Company CWAC

Addison Road
in winter blackout
seven a.m. and dawn
struggling through misty chimneys

we shuffle in the street
stretch out stiff arms in "Right dress"
to touch the next girl's sleeve
with its yellow maple leaf on brown —
"fried egg" badge of service overseas

then walk down Addison Road
past high walls lacking their iron gates
to Holland Park

Up the dark stairs to the office
where the sergeant-major gives us
the night's casualty cards
and we type cables
with particulars of wounds
sometimes imagining delivery of the news
to mothers, wives

more often thinking of getting off early
to the NAAFI at Notting Hill Gate
where Elizabeth Arden cosmetics
sell cheap to Canadian
service women

until it comes at last
the casualty card
for a friend

February 1945
A Birthday

A B-day
at 50 Company

we all go to the Knights of Columbus
then to the pub at Notting Hill

Smitty's twenty-two
getting married next week on leave
to a boy she's known three months
(no-one likes him, he's a *zombie*)

no permission from the army — it takes
too long — and Smitty's in a hurry
"I'm only half a virgin," Smitty says laughing
"I won't go all the way
till we're married."

Later drowned in beer tears
in her iron Addison Road bed
Smitty groans
"I'm pregnant."

"What a bed-pal, he's terrific!"
she tells us a month later
then cries over her mother's
joyful welcoming letter

February 1945
Viddy

Corporal Vidkoff of the Casualty Section
lately of St. Urbain Street
and the Quebec Padlock Law
has joined the British Communist party
goes to meetings every Wednesday night.

Viddy says his father
escaped to Canada in 1902
condemned to death in Czarist Russia
for stealing a horse to feed his family
"In Russia now," says Viddy, "everything
is for the people!"
then he does his famous imitation
of the Queen
struggling into her girdle
pulling elastic over bulges
stopping to scratch a bit —

We all like Viddy
so if the sergeant-major isn't looking
we give him the clenched fist
salute

March 1945
Chivalry

Whomp! the windows rattle
V2s exploding to the west
this one close enough to throw you
across the barrack box

the plane-tree's buds outside
are still locked in winter
and the mess gas-fire
warms three cubic feet of freezing air

yet these events occur:
last week, an orange each
an egg for breakfast,
spears of bulbs in the sooty garden

at the Haymarket Cinema
Henry the Fifth with trumpet fanfare
for those who
risk the nights in London

Intoxicated by Olivier's Harry
leading his happy few at Agincourt
on Crispin Crispian's day
we little band of comrades
float out into the blackout
rush for tube or bus.

At Holland Park a soldier
politely helps a Cwac alone
lighting the blackout with a shaded torch
while behind the garden walls of Addison Road
green lilacs quicken

April 1945
Violets

Working nights while armies
bomb their way across the Rhine
spending daytime off hours
wandering
Trafalgar Square, Westminster
where an American soldier
apple of some midwestern mother's eye
begs you to drink at the Strand Palace
complaining
of the high price of prostitutes

and you buy
yourself a bunch of Cornish violets

and later in the damp spaces
of the Casualty Section
stacked with records of the wounded and the dead
the violets spread their perfume from your jacket
round the dark room
inhabited now
only by Corporal Sutcliffe, and red-
mouthed civilian Gladys, who
doesn't believe you bought the violets for yourself,
recounts how she lost her
virginity at fourteen
to two artists she modelled for — then
disappears into the file room
with Sutty
while you read about Society weddings
in the *Sunday Mirror*.

April 1945
Romance

You've had his
glossy photograph
displayed and wonder
would you recognize him?
last seen in Montreal at the
Officers' Club
where you, a private, had to go in civvies

The girls of 50 Company
like his dark hair and
smile — though it's hard to
remember more
than the dance music at the
Normandie Roof

He writes from Halifax
about his corvette —
action stations
depth charges
submarines

different from your life:
the bus to Acton,
drafty Casualty Section,
listening to talk of *zombies*
laughing about last night's
hot-water-bottle —
blonde or brunette.

One day he walks into Records
asks the sergeant-major to let you off
because his ship's in Greenock
sails tomorrow.
You're Ingrid Bergman!
Luise Rainer!
in a movie called "Springtime"

A few
pre-war bulbs poke up in parks
wet sun shines on clouds
of pink almond blossom.
You jump on a big red bus together
sit on a side bench
holding hands

then stroll beside the Thames
watch a thick green tide
run out — he
buys you an etching of St. Paul's:
love-charm for the future.

Then a theatre
a terrible farce about
six vicars with George Gee —
remembered only because of
hard-held hands
warmth spreading through serge sleeves

Powdered-egg omelettes at Veeraswami's
before the night train to Scotland
where standing
squashed in the corridor
you talk of peace.

All the way back to London
you sleep
until a kind woman wakes you.

Numbness, misery.
You can't remember his voice or
touch until

imagination starts to work:
he shines again:
a photograph
you don't quite believe

May 1945
Telescope

I see Trafalgar Square
V.E. day —
that brilliant morning sun
the crowd gathering —
already a laughing queue
outside the bar
at the Captain's Cabin

at noon
the bells clash out.

In Downing Street
Churchill with cigar and V sign
at Buckingham Palace
the King, Queen and two princesses

all unseen by us
drinkers in the Captain's Cabin

Out of focus from so far
the day blurs
to gin, hot sun and laughter
until, back at Addison Road barracks
Kowalski at the switchboard
on duty by her own request
shrugs off V.E. day
telling about her American boyfriend
in the Pacific

then she pulls the blackout
since no one's told us not too —
and for her
the war's still on
and when I pull it back to see the stars
Kowalski rips it shut

November 1945
Auld Lang Syne

And so it's over
a last roll-call on the English dock
then filing up the long gangplank
to the decks of the *Isle de France*
where the Canadian Army plays crap

On the jammed ship
8 of us Cwacs share a small cabin
get 2 meals a day
sit on the floor of the grand salon
for lack of chairs
and swell the gift shop's roaring trade
in fake Chanel Number 5.

There's nothing much to think about
except reunions
and discharge from the army
perhaps no job

It's really best outside by day
bundling behind a funnel
with newly met old friends

Only
3 days back to Halifax
trains in slush on sidings
troops pouring out of the ship

We wait
listening to laments from a piper
pacing the seaward deck

and remember Aldershot
the last parade
marching feet
the CWAC band playing
Auld Lang Syne.

1952
Seven Years Later

shopping
prudently in Morgans
for a kiddy bed, a pressure cooker

wearing
a piece of silver fox
your aunt left you
and a little flowered hat

suddenly you see
Lafarge
across the furniture floor —
or is it?

that slatternly salesgirl
with sagging stomach
slack girdle
twisted ten-denier stockings and
draggled New Look skirt
those round shoulders
fizzy permanent wave —
it can't be

acid-tongued Lafarge
scourge of male stupidity at Headquarters
who typed Part 2 Orders
convulsed the Orderly Room with laughter
and drank with you V.E. day

you hurry over
anxious, smiling

and Lafarge's eyes
flick panicky recognition

before she walks away
in order not to serve you

Notes

Zombie was the derogatory slang term given by the volunteer Canadian Army (which included the CWAC) to soldiers conscripted under the National Resources Mobilization Act of 21 June 1942. Mackenzie King had promised then that the men were to be drafted to defend Canada only, and that they would never be sent overseas. In 1944 when the Canadian Army, fighting on the continent of Europe, was desperately short of reserves, King, under severe pressure from his cabinet, agreed to send the conscripts overseas.

Penicillin, newly discovered, was unavailable to civilians in 1944. Members of the armed services could and did receive it as treatment for severe infections.

PART 3 — A LAMP OF EARTH

The Warblers Come

At a signal of light
    the warblers come
I have seen them at the first silent
    spreading of leaves
gorging off poplar flowers, insects
    red elm danglers

More substantial than butterflies
    among green leaf balls
the warblers make currents
    in deep leaf water.

I hear their voices creaking
    glimpse scarlet, yellow, blue,
on foaming waves of leaves:
    and the warblers wings

flashing like buoys at night
    mark where safety lies
        and danger!

The Conquest Of Mexico — Montreal 1980

This Museum
is an encyclopedia
for the eye
a hive of artifacts
now petrified as dry tableaux
like a library of the dead
of wispy shadows
painted sticks and feathers
fixed in a desert of red clay

these animals, children, hunters, gods
are like so many rows of
stuffed chocolates
in a pastry shop
inviting gluttony
then cloying aftertaste

and at first
all the pots, jars, and plates
manikins and priestikins
choking in plexiglass cases,
jostling thousands of years
in the same prison,
burn with uniform hot terra cotta,
and numb my sensibility

then thinly
in the distance
a raucous music sounds
like a carnival beginning
at the far end of the street
where a jester caracoles and screams
in front of a delicately plodding
mild white bull
pulled by painted devils
trailing flowers

and with a roar the people of Yucatan
dance for me
under their capes of jaguar —
jaguar's legs hanging round
their own, and dancing too.

And the shadows burst
into sunlight
up the steps of the temples
first seen in my mother's heavy
mulberry-coloured volumes
of the Conquest of Mexico —
when I joined the parade of black emblems
of Montezuma's courtiers
flaunting the banners and flowers,
as I turned the pages of Prescott
half-listening to my mother
reading to my brother
while in the great vase of delphiniums
filling the dead fireplace
live bees worked.

Bulbs

1. Bulb With A Future

It's
almost
too late to
plant pink earlies
now that frost hardens
earth where you left a few
riotous geraniums no heart to
tear them up to make room for
fancies of the season
after the next one
just the same
I'll do it

2. Another Bulb

comic
strip
ideas
are lit
bulbs over
the heads of
characters about to
outwit authority or invent
absurdity which may illuminate
with inked rays spreading the word
to hang in bubbles above the others'
heads something about our human
condition in the eighties.
l t
i h
k i
e s

Marmalade

Thinking of marmalade

I remember my father scooping
mounds of it onto his bread
like that illustration for the Hillair Belloc poem —
a man with stubble chin
napkin tied round thick neck,
bliss apparent
in square eyes and teeth
sinking into a doorstep of bread —
and shovelling marmalade in.

Making marmalade:
not that cloying conserve of
sunkist, grapefruit, lemon, but
marmalade made from
beautiful bitter Sevilles.

Marmalade: the pungent
smell, the chickling pan,
sore arches and
stiff arm from stirring —
scrape of spoon on metal
then the test on a cold saucer
fingering syrup onto the tongue:

storing jars
in a cool cupboard
rows of dark orange suns
waiting to light up
winter's breakfast table.

First Time In The West

First time in the West
and taking Instamatic snaps of
plum trees, yellow gorse and broom
M.G.s and bug-eyed Sprites
roaring to the beaches

Gas Town under steam then
vast quadrangles of Simon Fraser
enclosing
scarlet corridors and
library — wired like an aviary

Your office
pneumatic with cream plastic,
telephones asprout with buttons
connecting you to
power in Ottawa
your sister

You show me China Town
Dim Sum off a formica table
while a brace of chefs
juggle their cleavers
under a duck curtain
pressed in an Eastern mould
like me.

Your hired Cessna
grinds across Saltspring,
pale green trees
look like bright lichen cups
open

and smaller islands
bask like crocodiles

with log-strewn beaches
lakes growing lily pads of rafts
and mountains of Vancouver Island
ring-wormed with logging roads

Watching Canada's
other edge below
I hate my thick skin
barnacled with
language, custom, old
grudges.

Settlement

I've heard it said that solitude's joy
is the other face of depression
that for every thrill of freedom
there is payment,
that only partnership brings pure happiness,
that the spreading warmth of the other in a bed,
the stirring, the movements toward
or even away, confirm you in life and blood.

But those same movements tangle up
the long threads of thought
that might have wound in memories
in meditation —
that hand, exploring, knots
imagination, brought up short
against the heavy anchor of the other,
even if it's groping
only to be sure you're there.

Yet you who are
always on the brink of a voyage
have you ever been close to leaving?
if every obstacle had melted
would you have stepped
into the ship
with silver wings?
or have all your mutterings been
only the sound of the earth settling?

A Lamp Of Earth

I search for the boletus
watching the pine needles of the island floor
for glowing red-brown humps
leaning together in rings

I take a sharp-edged clamshell
and cut the boletus' stem just below
the tattered ring of hymen,
the stem flushes purple,
deep holes run to its centre
where insects have devoured the rich flesh.

Another boletus in the spore-ring
domed, golden, shining,
like a wet beach stone —
I cut with my clamshell
the underside is dewy, whole,
pores stippled like a mediterranean sponge,
I hold it carefully in my palm.

At night we eat boletus —
they taste of lemons
but are not fruits of sunshine —
they are lamps of earth.

Lines Written In Dejection In Kingston Station

Waiting
stifling
in Kingston Station
edges blunted
by VIA's chimes and
amplified announcements —
better two hours late than
never.

Tinted windows
against the sun reveal
far down the track
a train approaching at funeral pace
with attendant mourners
carrying shovels —

slowly the cortege
grinds forward
dashing a last desperate hope it's the
Rapido —
and with hellish rumble
hoppers open
pouring onto the track
heavy black gravel.

Here we are
suspended
between hope and rebellion.
Thus do our masters
ensure our
stability.

Digging The Glads

Brown spears of gladiolus
lean in all directions
under remembered weight of
sweet-smelling flowers

and frost's dark nails
have scratched the thick leaves of
this one that was crimson, that one
yellow and scarlet with
flaring petals' ruffled edges
peaked over a mouth
inviting bees

My fork breaks hard ground
cracking it open until
the corms click out of it
pink like just-peeled mackintosh apples
and pebbles of new corms sprinkle
blackened marigolds

Shaking earth from fat siamese twins
prying off last summer's
shrivelled old wart
I smell
decay and growth

and remember the gladiolus
my dear aunt grew
each summer
flowers opening
one above the other
frilled and edged with colours of a
Duffy painting
vibrant
all singing a heavenly anthem
in time together

Trout Stream

Susanna Moodie's Reverie — 1882

When we came to the old woman's house
I knew it was much too small
daylight showed between logs
we nailed up windows with white cloth
against rain.
But a brook ran
beside a rise where the cabin stood,
trout lazed in the shallows:
orange spots against pebbles, opening
mouths swallowing, swallowing,
reflecting from their backs
the sky colours.
Even in winter
the fish spoke under thick ice.

We all squeezed into the cabin,
husband, baby, maidservant, manservant
listening to each others movements in the long nights.

Yankee neighbours, here for cheap land
(more likely to keep out of jail)
jeered at my careful speech
borrowed my food and thread,
whisky and oven,
took the plough and
gave it back broken,
came to help build a barn
then gorged and drank till dawn
shouting lewd songs, vomiting in corners,
made other nights terrible with shivarees
when old men married to young brides
were taunted
and tarred and feathered.

Yet when our cabin burned
on a night cracking with cold
Yankee neighbours took us in,
put the baby to sleep in a dresser drawer,
gave us beds and hot food

I, a lady, learned
the lessons of chapped hands,
servants gone, a husband serving the Colours.

Ah, but my brook ran on
all those winters —
all year, for years — the fish
swam lazily
here and at Otonabee.

Once my new speckled trout
gasping for gentler air
pointed east for home,
now they are fat, enamelled and glittering,
jewelled with summer suns
they drowse in warm shallows

my fish thoughts
swim to paper.

PART 4 — GOOD-BYE TO THE SUGAR REFINERY

Moving West

Often we parked on the street to the east of the hall
walked down beside the red-roofed church where
the family were all christened
even after the congregation had moved West.

Symphony night was Wednesday —
not the fashionable night when people went
to be seen, but the other night.

The hall sat squat like a space ship and we went in
through the back entrance
and were suddenly thrown into light and pictures
and talk and the buzz of crowds riding escalators

under armadillo-plated lamps
we crossed a crimson carpet
took another escalator, or two, up, up
to our seats in the top balcony
at the extreme end
at the back —
(my friend has claustrophobia
and as well
is afraid of falling over the edge)

Strangely enough
these are the best seats in the house
for hearing
and sometimes the Gazette critic
takes them from us.

Already
the orchestra makes
strange noises,
clatters its music stands
in front of grey screens that might be
backdrop to a Beckett play

We've read the program
I'm ready to fall over the edge
and the concert begins.
We sit here in ecstasy
not knowing
we'll soon go West
ourselves.

Incommunicado

Suburbia —
large lots
mown grass but no flowers
half an acre of
owned woods

executive
bay-windowed, heat-efficient
indoor-outdoor mainfloor
families
cowering behind
two-car garages —
where

darkness of summer leaves
shades the neighbours'
cluster of mailboxes
threatening

from the outer world of
terrorists
welfare recipients
rapists and muggers

communication.

Crossroads

At a crossroads in Bermuda
a tall Quebec spruce
glows with coloured lights,
glitters fake icicles

hibiscus and oleander flame amongst
banyans
warm ocean rain
runs from thick leaves to
crabgrass speared with daffodils

whistles shrill
to throbbing kettle drums —
Gombey dancers
whirl into the crossroads
wearing magic
sprays of peacocks' feathers
tall reed hats
shirts flashing mirrors, ribbons,
the leader in a horrid mask
wielding a plastic axe.

Canada in Bermuda:
a few military graves looking west
a few millionaires,
insurance men,

and this spruce tree
that might remind you
of a Quebec Christmas cracking with cold
when even the wine for the *réveillon*
froze in the woodshed

and on Christmas morning
skiing uphill to the village
through six feet of snow
we were all soon as hot as
Gombey dancers

“That spruce tree,” I ask you,
“Does it make you think of home?”

“That’s my new mast,” you say.

Vos Phares — Your Headlights

hotly arguing
right up to the Trans-Canadian
and the south turn-off
to Lachine, the Champlain Bridge
and the Eastern Townships

arguing as we surged underground
into the dark tunnel
where a river of yellow lights swept past
with a roar and high-pitched whine of tires

then, sunlight again, and a sign:

Vos Phares?

and we argued on
past the mounts of St. Bruno and St. Hilaire
while the Green Mountains of Vermont
scalloped the horizon
and the road at last began
to rise and fall
beside Owl's Head and Orford

we argued right
down the forgotten east shore
of Lake Memphramagog
where Loyalists' descendants even now
won't speak French

and suddenly saw
our headlights
still lit.

Youghall Beach

Walking from the farm
past Ingle Neuk boarding-house
to the long sands
where children darted like insects
and splashed in ocean pools
we sniffed the heavy sulfur air from Bathurst
talked of rain next day
when the children might ride
old Charlie, the farm workhorse
(the small ones sitting in front of Dave)
or watch Mrs. Hogan, up to the elbows in a
great bowl of flour
work the dough
slap it onto the scrubbed wooden table
knead it with a hissing noise
"Feels like a warm wet baby," she'd say
looking out of the corners of her eyes
as her daughters, student nurses, home
to help with the summer boarders
yanked black pans of squares from the
wood-fired range

On the porch
the two old ladies from Montreal would be on the slider
(Miss Christie from Burton's bookshop and her sister)
watching rain
complaining about holes in the fly-screens
children locked in the only bathroom
reading comics — but
Miss Christie and her sister
would never go anywhere else

Next year everything was different.
Mr. Hogan drove a new bright red station wagon.
The farm had been painted and
fixed up.

In the evening he told us Mrs. Hogan had died
showed us her Lieutenant-Governor's medal
won in nineteen thirty-six
for the highest school leaving mark in New Brunswick

He wiped his eyes
he missed her — but

we never went back.

Good-bye To The Sugar Refinery

Have you ever seen a wall swaying,
grappling hook like leaches
sucking its top
long lines snaking
to the ground
Can you imagine the wall floodlit?
like a liner leaving a dock
with streamers looping to shore?
Imagine the sugar factory behind the wall
exploding
throwing bricks all over the street
and all the toilets running golden syrup
till the floors fell in from shock.
And strange things happened: a man
running away
broke his ankle —
died of drugs meant to save him.
And the pigeons
that used to live in the sugar warehouse
huddled on the ground — talking English
and migrating rats
were seen in the streets
consulting
and the factory cats
rubbed up against strangers.

That wall didn't fall down all at once.
But at last it flew into pieces —
disappeared with a roar
in a cloud of nineteenth
century dust.

Shrinking Patterns

Red October's patterns
shrink to dun and motley.

Oak leaves etched with rust make
green grass a persian carpet
of tobacco and dried blood.

Evening primroses
semaphore downwards
between rusty berries and wild
asparagus feathers
towards the waiting earth.

Each day smaller
the Kinglet's eye ring
blinks from the yellow hedge.
He's sheathed his scarlet crest for the long flight.
Only tortoiseshell sparrows
keep life going.

Dorothy's Song

. . . Afterwards William lay, and I lay in the trench under the fence — he with his eyes shut and listening to the waterfalls and the Birds . . . William heard me breathing and rustling now and then but we both lay still, and unseen by one another. He thought it would be sweet thus to lie so in the grave . . .

Dorothy Wordsworth's Diary
Thursday 29 April 1802

My love and I lie on the ground
Leaves curl in my ear
his breath moves my hair
a pale orchid like a tulip
grows by my eye.
His long body
lies against mine.

A buzzard slides
on the wind
in the wheeling sky
as I slide to nowhere.

Clouds bearing Nobodaddy
growl out of the north
but we roll with
the rolling
earth   fall
with the
fell's waterfalls
while sheep lament
lapwings cry.

The juice runs out in the becks
the warm ground sweats.
Here in the ditch we lie —
my love and I.